Blood Flower

Other works by Pamela Uschuk:

Poetry:

Finding Peaches in the Desert

One-Legged Dancer

Scattered Risks

Without the Comfort of Stars

Crazy Love
(American Book Award)

Wild in the Plaza of Memory

and numerous chapbooks

Blood Flower

New Poems

Pamela Uschuk

WingsPress

San Antonio, Texas
2015

Blood Flower © 2015 by Pamela Uschuk

Cover painting: "The Waltz" by Judi Uschuk-Stahl.
Used by permission of the artist.

ISBN: 978-1-60940-411-6 (paperback original)

E-books:

ePub: 978-1-60940-412-3
Mobipocket/Kindle: 978-1-60940-413-0
Library PDF: 978-1-60940-414-7

Wings Press
627 E. Guenther
San Antonio, Texas 78210
Phone/fax: (210) 271-7805
On-line catalogue and ordering:
www.wingspress.com

Wings Press books are distributed to the trade by
Independent Publishers Group
www.ipgbook.com

Cataloging In Publication:

Uschuk, Pamela.
  [Poems. Selections]
  Blood flower : new poems / Pamela Uschuk.
    pages ; cm
  ISBN 978-1-60940-411-6 (pbk. : alk. paper) -- ISBN 978-1-
60940-412-3 (epub ebook) -- ISBN 978-1-60940-413-0 (kindle-
mobipocket ebook) -- ISBN 978-1-60940-414-7 (library pdf
ebook)
  I. Title.
  PS3571.S38A6 2015
  811'.54--dc23
                                    2014034441

Blood Flower *is dedicated with love and healing
to all my family who have passed from this planet,
but, most of all, it is dedicated to my sisters,
Judi Uschuk-Stahl and Val Uschuk,
my fierce and necessary companions
on this long journey.*

*It is also dedicated to Kasia Sokol-Borup,
my adopted Polish sister, without whose music
this book would not have reached such high notes.*

*And, finally, it is dedicated to Bill Root,
husband, lover and fellow adventurer,
who I still madly love after all these years.*

*I would also like to acknowledge my dear friends,
Joy Harjo, who gave me critical suggestions about
these poems in their infancy, and Terry Acevedo,
who has listened to so many of these poems
as they were being crafted.*

*Thank you to all my ancestors who came before,
and, without whom, there would be no stories.*

CONTENTS

Blood Flower

The Trick

Talk About Your Bad Girls

Blood Flower

"To cleanse my eyes, my mouth, my ears
of all that drifted on the wind.
I dream my blouse becomes
like powdered snow upon my back."

—Yunna Morits

A SIBERIAN COLD FRONT TAKES OVER THE LAST WEEK OF APRIL

Siberia, I do not need your sleet today,
impaling me like a fork in a cheek.
Not that you don't feel free to crowd my life with ancestors,
memories of bear paws and shrill white distances
cracking the civilized seams of my brain.
Today, Siberia, my head aches with your steel humidity,
cold as a slug's mucous skirts,
slick as the stone pipe of a shamanka.
I'd like to refuse your telegram.
I am not the she-bear taken as wife by a man.
I will not give birth to the bear boy hero
who'll save the tribe.
Take back your message
to the grandmothers who poke at the ashes
of my beginning-of-the-century thoughts.
Tell them to pack their travois of Arctic wind
and haul away the dull gray blades of these clouds.
Hurry on. Skip my generation of stars.
At the lip of spring
chapped by your kisses,
the numb thud of your heart stunning wisteria, tulips,
the bulging red buds of peonies,
time is short.
I fall daily in love with impossibilities—
the screech owl flying in front of the new moon,
the rufus hummingbird who puffs his throat
like a lung of electric carnelian
through the window,

the man shaped like a grizzly bear,
but I know that
just as I feel my womb contract
troops are massing on the other side of the globe
for another war
too quick for even their long talons to stop.

RED MENACE

for my family

Now I know why teachers refused
to pronounce my name.
They knew.
In their very simplest syllables,
they knew—
Jones, Pierce, Drew—
Russian rides roughshod,
a Tartar horseman across
the tongue, dances
tranced as the bear
Siberian shamans become.
Too many consonants befuddle,
breed fear in the ear
of the English-speaking host.
Even our alphabet's a schism
intoned by Orthodox priests
with long white beards, half-pagan,
signing their backward cross.

It's in our blood, high
cheekbones, unbobbed noses,
the only ones in our small Midwest town—little Ruskies!
Teachers and classmates called us
Commies for a joke,
              so I learned
"Wait till we take over the world!"
For that, I was deported
to the empty hall
or the principal with shaved eyebrows.

What was a Commie to me?
A bear painted red, sickle
on his forehead, missiles
pointed at America's vulnerable heart
where I, too, lived?

My father farmed like the Germans
who surrounded us, like the Swedes
down the road and the English
who owned most of those
flat Michigan fields.

"Foreigner. Half-wild." they said,
when down the runaway road
my father ran after our mad bull, Ike,
then grabbed the lead rope.
With a punch solid
between the bellowing eyes,
father stunned Ike docile.
Just what they feared.

When they painted *Red, Commie Bastard*
on my father's machines,
it hurt us all.
An Air Corps hero
in both theatres
of the Second World War,
this man who refused to sign
McCarthy's loyalty oath
taught us to salute the flag.
In school, they tried—
I give them that—
to take the Russian
out of my head.

But my cheekbones knew
and my tongue's Cyrillic rhythms
and my heart
with its rebellious beat.

Movies were the final straw—
films clicking like locusts
through the afternoon
doze of history class, listing
the dangers of becoming a Red.
Your family would be stoned, your father
locked up, your mother
sent to die in a psychiatric ward.
Every time, the children shamed.
At the sorry end of the show, Commie kids
stood alone, orphaned
with the Star Spangled Banner
snapping over their heads.

I was no Red, no Commie
but I loved borscht, Tolstoy
and the Bolshoi ballet,
adored the Slavic way
Grandma rolled her r's,
her Oriental eyes
and Indian face.

After all these years
it's clear what it was
those teachers couldn't name—
not just the consonants
but the roots,
      the skin drums,

feathers hung
    from the horse's manes,
the gypsy gait
    of the troika over snow,
icon candles
    dripping and thick,
the longing for the sky
    wide above the Steppes.

I forgive them, forgive them all.
They didn't think but to accuse
what is oldest in us.
I give them back
their colonial history
and Republican votes,
their medium-range words against fear.
They will never learn
to pronounce our allegiance
to what survives,
        a wilderness of passion
thicker than the veneer of a few hundred years
charging our blood
    red and free.

BLACK SWAN

Inside the photo's tapestry, your silk sleeves
don't reveal the slit wrists of madness
or the raw cortex of gang legends I loved—
police bullets slugging your car's backseat
over my father's young head as you ran
whiskey from Canada for the Purple Gang.
No one talks about your stints
in Joliet and Jackson Prison after you roped
concrete to a corpse you sank in the Grand River.

Who was he, Grandfather?
I feel cheated. *Kto vui?*
Who are you? I cannot find
your pauper's grave.

Like Bogart's in a film noir
your mouth is a tight-set scar.
Did it elide vowels
fluid as trout in a cold stream
tearful over the Firebird's Tale, or sneer
remembering your father's ultimatum—
        leave Russia or join the Tsar's army—
after your tantrum murdered his valet?

Charming pariah pitched across the Atlantic's green remorse,
you vowed to send back your first son. But,
what promise did you ever keep?
Ellis Island misspelled your name,

deloused you like everyone else.
Russian was the official language
in your American house built with secret
hideaways beneath hollow attic steps, false
bedroom walls. Still, you tithed
gang money to Orthodox priests.

Grandfather, what purpose can you discern
now your entitled eyes are soil,
your heart going to anthracite?
Through the ghosts of your manicured hands
that never picked up a hammer
pierce my curious roots.

Even in this distant pose, you glide,
the gorgeous black swan who rules
with stiff wings curled
terrorizing, above a charred back,
mallards with his hiss—
irresistable bully of the pond.

Cursed by indelible longing
for birch groves, balalaikas, whirling
Mazurkas, despite a day like today when the earth sinks
to its hips in the rare currency of peace, when
chickadees and finches bask
in the season's final leaf-lit fling,
when squirrels nap after cannonballing
walnuts to the yard, when
nothing,
            nothing in particular
disturbs one molecule of the afternoon,
you smothered your future in Grandma's yellow kitchen.

What is it in this decaying loam
that makes me cry? What impossible longing,
deformed as swallows reflected in a gazing globe,
when sun seems to illuminate the most stubborn shade?
The same chink in the genes?

Ya Ruskaya, Grandfather; look at the icons I keep—
an inlaid jewelry box from Siberia,
Minsk enameled knives,
the Orthodox cross or your portrait
arranged before the samovar
I carry from house to house.

'33, did you die in '33, syllables
shrill as ax blades sunk into a maple tree,
the same number as your savior's age
when he was crucified? *Horosho.*

Grandfather, tell me what fist beat
blue as lacy veins
trapped in our temples,
when you reached for the oven door,
blew out the pilot
                    to suffocate our lives?

BREWING BORSCHT

for Anna Jackinchuk

I cube chunks of slick beef,
slippery meat I toss to werewolves in the pan
where garlic shimmies and steams
in rosemary, fresh feathery dill.
The beets are crisp, green
stalks held high, a bouquet I deliver
like Marie Antoinette's stiff collars
to the chopping block.

Oh, to palm the red cabbage head
the way my grandmother must have cupped
my infant skull while she laughed,
so wrinkled she dubbed me Prune,
her honey girl. I am
in her kitchen again, lemon
with white sills and an enormous stove
where she cooked borscht,
vareniki, peroghi, apple
fritters, rich duck blood soup,
where she learned to share food
with the wolves of sorrow
the heartsick afternoon
her handsome husband took his life,
fragrant suicide in her oven.

I am making borscht today
absurd though it is in desert heat
to steam the heart of my kitchen
with this savory soup of memories.

Somewhere outside Prague, my great-grandmother
unfurls her auburn mane,
purrs, half-closes her almond eyes
after stirring the flame
under the smoky pot where she's chopped
roots from her winter cellar—
carrots, beets, then the shank of spring lamb
that mouthed their tender leaves.

When I cut beets, the platelets of centuries
flow from their concentric rings
staining my hands.
I marvel at how we fit like *Matryoshka* dolls
inside each other's lives—
Grandma, Great-grandmother,
and me brewing borscht thick as mating musk
to heal all grief, to wake
this house from fitful dreams.

WILDFLOWERS

for Anna Petroska Jackinchuk (1894-1983)

I

I arrange cornflowers, brown-eyed Susans,
roadside purple rockets—
decades since you taught me their names.
        You said wind scoured words from your head,
blowing stronger each year.

Grandma, how completely your stories flew me
to the old country, red poppies and mountains
blue as aging veins, cures boiled from mushrooms,
        and the times, coming home late, you hid
in river willows
        spying on a gypsy camp.
Dreaming of perfect love, you hugged your knees against
cold and rocked to balalaikas
and guitars carved from trees of flame,
dancing like icons in your mother's bedroom.

That dark pulse caught you early
when, instead of capping beer in the family brewery,
you climbed onto blocks of straw-covered ice
and twirled until you flipped
head-first to the skidding floor.
Unconscious days you dreamed
you were a wren tossed inside a storm..
When you woke, the wind began.

Did you think it was penance
that your mother sent you alone
and knowing no English
to be saved by America?
        Your sole welcome to Ellis Island
were gusting Atlantic waves and a cousin
who sold you to a sweat shop.

II

In Philadelphia you rolled cigars
then fled, strange wren, to sing
and dance in carnivals until you saw Grandfather's
fire-black eyes in his charmed face.
High-stepping, he was
your fairy tale Russian prince.

Remember yellow roses, amethyst
lilacs, kiss-me-over-the-garden-gate?
Their petals held no alien voice
but became the fluid language
you composed into a garden
when Grandfather betrayed
his promises of faith and lace.

Even as you planted the Peace Rose,
packing black soil around its waxy trunk,
he bootlegged whiskey from Canada,
bought long black sedans
and pearl-studded suits to win
women whose rouged faces
you weeded from nightmares.

His manic laughter was prohibition
that kept you at the stove over borscht,
babka, duck blood soup.
                              How you hated to sing
and dance for his Purple Gang friends.
That bloody mob packed
the false walls of your house
with whiskey and bathtub gin, used your sons
as mannequins to foil police.

My favorite story is the final time
that Grandfather met you
at the front door, taut leather strap
slapping his palm as you led your kids
back from the Saturday matinee.
Over the porch rail you shattered
a milk bottle, whispering
              No sir, Mister, now things must change.

Broken glass striping his throat, he
dropped the belt, and from that day
you passed untouched.
After, you took in bushels of laundry,
mopped rich oak floors so you could buy
bread with your independent coins.
By that sweet rebellion
your children were fed.

Bullets tore the roots from your dreams
those long months Grandfather was shuttled
to prison for a murder no one could prove.
              On his last parole he beat
your oldest son, my father, then
backhanded him through the bleeding porch window.

His furious screams could no longer order
his son back to the terrified house.

Hours before you got off work
Grandfather locked the kitchen doors,
blew out the pilot,
and gassed his frost-bitten sorrow
in your stove.

III

Is it any surprise you warned me
about men? Like all warriors,
you stood your own ground, even
the time your second husband was so drunk
he couldn't recall
how whiskey drove anger
          when he split the kitchen table top
with a cleaver meant for you.
          Mowing the lawn he cut
the plush tongues of snapdragons,
fragile moss rose,
snow-on-the-mountain,
cursing stems and petals clogging his blades.

Complaints were as foreign as I would become to you.
Memorizing your hands, weightless
and resilient as bird bones,
I came to say goodbye
You pointed to the magnolia opening the yard
with blossoms healing as your absolute laughter.

So far north, you marveled
it survived so many winters
when hardier plants died.
I told you I was flying to mountains
I'd never seen, knowing
I had to cultivate other ground.
When I tried to talk you into coming along
you repeated,
>   *Wildflowers can't be transplanted.*
>   *I want to die in my own house.*

Grandma, you loved best
dark petals,
>   black marooned roses,
cinnamon deep azaleas.
The richest you fixed in my hair.
I still can't turn from your blue eyes
that tend a garden I could own.

There is no sound as loud as
this passing when you waved through the screen,
>   *I'll see you in the clouds*
>   *when the wind stops.*

ANOTHER EASTER SNOWSTORM

for Teresa Acevedo and Lorian Hemingway

Fire in the wood stove doesn't snap so much
as whine against this April storm.
I wince at chunks of snow clotting pines,
the vulnerable new leaves
of the copper rose. Downstairs
La Virgen de Guadalupe smudges
Easter eve, rolls her eyes
in disbelief at this surfeit of white.
Her memory fastens on
crucifix-shaped cacti, the thin arms
of the camposino with a machete
she blinded in a field of maguey.

Nose in his tail, the white wolf
is the question mark of a ghost
praying for the resurrection of the sun.
In his world there is no sin
to run from, just the body
and blood of the deer
wholly in his belly.

Snow drops love notes from the dead
no one wants yet to open. Did I ever feel
renewal at Easter or was it always
just another knock knock rabbit joke,
jelly beans, fake grass in baskets,
dyeing eggs, our arms and dog paws,
the only time besides Christmas
that mom made us go to church?

What I remember of redemption was ham
and new potatoes with dill, the funeral
smell of hyacinth and tulips
with their unyeilding lips, and the way
Christ's wounds terrified the day,
the storm of bloody thorns and nails
ordained by a father who thundered
punishment, not love. I was confused
by the frail architecture of grace.

I remember my grandma would slip
a twenty into my palm, feed
me chocolate-covered orange rinds,
tell me again about picking mushrooms
in the Carpathian Mountains, the way
her mother's eyes rolled after she ran
to the river to listen to gypsies sing,
the way she'd have to confess to the priest
who would later try to rape her.
When she told me she escaped, Easter
seemed almost real.

NIGHT TERRORS

for my brother, John

> "Vaste est la maison qui m'écrase."
> —Berber Proverb

What breathes between the dawn death of stars
reeks like wood smoke caught
in the guard hairs of a mule deer
stepping through Arctic carcasses of hail
spewed by a thunderstorm's last gash.

Sorrow's red road opened
in night terrors remembering
my brother who at three reached out
to wriggle his fingers
into the socket in our parent's bedroom.
Razors of blue flame
knocked him into my screech
until nothing but the black horse of stun
reared to kick the life from both of us.

Where were our parents? Arguing
over egg money or the broken Sears lawn mower
they'd forget by morning, their breathing
wobbly as bottles of Blatz beer
chinking the formica kitchen table
while we comforted our own tears
searing cigarette holes
into the bare arms of our discoveries?

What breathes between stars
is buried in the plastic cans
of Mom's and Dad's ashes secured
now under the piñons in the yard.
How slow the aftershock of memory, the stink
of fingertips charred by the stark
yap of amped volts sparking
our parents' angry screams at our stupidity
when we ran to them for help.

Even at four, I gauged electricity as a kind of song—*take*
care of yourself syllables that gnawed
through the wires of my childhood.

What breathes between stars is sticky
as an orb weaver's web, as last fall's bottle fly
resurrected to flight, as smoky as the mule deer
disappearing between the junipers of memory,
leading her new fawns
beyond the mountain lion's stone den.

RED CAT NEAR OLD SNOW

I used what was left of a burned matchstick and wrote on
a bar of soap in my cell. I would read it and read it
until it was committed to memory. Then with one
washing of my hands it would be gone.

—Irina Ratushinskaya,
Soviet dissident poet

In the milk-shuttered light of knowing
what's to come, of being
          what's passed before,
snow is shorn close to ice, fire sinks in the stove.

          No breezed branches,
just locks and the cat, red tabby,
          its white patches passing like snow.

In sun, he rubs
          against my calf,
dreams his claws
          in a warbler's throat.

Under river ice, the slow current fingers stones,
          silt puffing like clams blowing,
takes carp and their common cargo of gold
          despised by the sportsman's line,
to riversmeet, then to the sea
washing blood from the City's shores.
Each March, runoff is the tyrant that collapses bridges
          wherever it goes.

Spring is the dream of the self
split by the Dogwood bud,
          ruby Tag Alders that peel back to green,
to the fragile white petal of desire.

You are a moon inside bars,
a new Cerulean Warbler in the cat's moon eyes.
The old country seduces
but matchsticks char my plans.

What begins the wren?
How does the bear end?

The soap is hard, holds
passion frothing in ash.
How chapped those hands!

Under ice, the river blows
the old husk of Dogwood to silt.
And the cat, from shadow
to shadow, washes prey
from its chameleon coat.

LEARNING THE THEREMIN

for Steve Romaniello

This instrument looks like the black box salvaged
from a downed Russian jet except for the halo
tube at one end to modulate tones
eerie as whale song or the elastic
booming of outer space.
Leave it to my people to invent music
replicating the songs of ghosts rising
from Stalingrad's mass graves
or the long starved bones of poets
and physicists exiled by Stalin's torture squads
to die in Siberia.   With its own bizarre ethos,
this instrument is a heart too sensitive to be touched.
When Steve plays "Over The Rainbow"
with one vibrating fist aimed at its antennae
and the other hand spread, levitating
above the halo, Judy Garland warbles vowels
from her tomb, and our bodies resonate
like moonstung swamp reeds or like
skulls pelted by meteors until they crack
open to let in a spectral summons
we'd rather forget. Who could bear
to listen to an entire concert
tinged with blind eye sockets, the hinged
ends of charred arm bones, grave stones
slick with moss erasing epitaphs and names?
This music lacks blood in the same way
a cobra's eye ices as it charms
it's victim before it strikes.

But, as Steve's hands mesmerize the invisible,
conjuring those quavering notes
from the quickened air between us, we
cannot move away, sucked by inevitability
between constellations
into black holes of longing
mapping each of our cells.

SHOSTAKOVICH: FIVE PIECES
FOR VIOLIN AND CELLO

For Kasia Sokol

PRELUDE

There is never enough grain
in winter for the horses or mothers
without coats, and even while the samovar
empties the weak tea of party loyalty
into cracked glasses, there is one lump of sugar
written by the hands of the composer
who creates true notes blue
as damp wood smoke
choking St Petersburg, notes Stalin
slaps at with his iron fist.

GAVOTE

It's the Russian in me that charges out
in my dark velvet skirts, heart
as blood-gorged as Anna's watching
the train gain speed for her leap, when I hear
what your violin remembers
so that troikas pulled by those
wild-muscled Siberian stallions
rip through my snowy birch woods, nearly
trampling me to the death I need.

ELEGY

There can be no poetry
or music without lilies or bullets,
the frail lace of birch bark peeling
under a tyrant's arthritic hands.
This is the history of my people, the hope
of barley going gold on vast steppes
and the underground arteries
of potato vines sacrificed to worms.
In my greatgrandfather's house,
the ghosts of brushes and oil paint,
a potter's wheel, leather-
bound books of poems black with mold,
broken tea glasses, a balalaika's
grief, a bent samovar, and somewhere
under dust, the whip my grandfather used
to kill the servant who angered him.

WALTZ

Did Stalin long for water or the shore?
For leaves or waves to fill
the boat that would carry him
from his insomnia, his terror
of surgery, his temper smashing
every glass in his tower?
This waltz crawls up the violin's throat
while your wrist flexes
graceful as the neck of the Phoenix
regarding ashes. Who understands
the Firebird better than
those who have been betrayed?

Lean into the arms of these whole notes,
bury your lips in the neck of what would devour you
as you sashay away from the noose.

POLKA

Nothing understands the ecstatic wine
of this music like your body
dipping its oar into dark currents
then stretching on toe tips
to suicidal high notes.
Some music is wind, some
cherry wood flames fed
by blonde sticks of birch
crackling a St. Petersburg stove.
We survive snow to eat pear blossoms
on a gray April evening when the bow
smokes through each chord
that would sink our houses in grief.

Kasia, since you were sixteen, your violin
has been compass, tormentor
and lover. Tonight your strings
raise Shostakovich from the dead,
his white lips on fire, this
music, lilies and bullets
divined from our winter souls.

IRON AND LACE

for Katarzyna Sokol

I

Across the butt of a violin that scars her neck
with raw-mouthed wounds, Kasia
smooths a soft white cloth

           before Bach seizes her strings
squeezes air from the hall, quickening us
to believe in the wet dreams of blossoms, sweet
agony of tulips slashed by rain
or cliff swallows taking needles of twilight
into their open beaks, stitching
sky's ripped hem.

Each note's small coal singes our wrists.
Oh, to know the jagged brink of beauty
is to touch the white teeth of madness
and the fine art of licking blades in dark rooms.

II

Silk flame, she dares
the heart of mahogany desire.
Silver-sequined, her skin flickers
smooth as olive oil, lips
swollen Polish cherries,
this symphony loving the length of her body

as it is consumed
in snowlight,
starswoon,
the full moons of our broken hearts,
transforming ennui to soul shrieks of terror and joy.

Astromerea and white mums,
red velvet vulva of roses
                hum in the humming light
as this music lifts only to drop us
        shattering like crystal glasses
        thrown onto the stone cold hearth of alone.

What we inhale is strangled
as the breathing of horses in a winter pasture.

III

The second movement begs us not to die.
        Music of our grandmothers, notes
thick as birthblood on white sheets,
sharp as the crack of firing squad rifles,
whispy as the swish of scythes
in Slavic fields of barley and black rye buzzed by bees.

Music of our grandfathers, stern
as ice on birch trees, soft
as their hands in drawing rooms, crazing new snow
under sleighs, the thrum of running hooves.

Didn't our grandmothers cry as they lit candles
left in winter windows dazed by Baltic wind,

melting before icons of saints
who forgot to answer prayers
or intercede on behalf of sunlight
to save land licked by sky's gray tongue?

Bach, and the bow skates across strings, their
                              ache echoing between
comets written in the cold space above the heart.

IV

When a woman makes music, leaves
swing and the flights of larks
alter as they wing above cattails
and the buds of chestnut trees.

When a woman makes music, the course
of the river shimmies
free of ice as passionate stones
unbury their long grief.

When a woman plays music, small bones
in the wrist ache, and the necks
of crocuses crack
underground.

When a woman makes music, glass
windchimes of fortune ring ecstatic in wind,
toss black roses on bedcovers with each deep tone.

V

If air could speak, it would be most articulate
in the pleading of high C. Who among us
can resist sorrow borne by an extra string?
What collarbone can hold the galaxy of such need?

Does the flame understand
the lead weight of light it casts to shadow?

Even the fragile lips of astromerea open
moist as iceshine, swollen
as flooded loam, breastbone and pelvis
tumescent while skulls
empty themselves to night's calyx.

VI

It is as if a flock of hummingbirds
has swarmed into the concert hall, begging
forgiveness from the mouths of trumpet flowers
whose nectar they drink to live.

When Kasia plays, stars hold their breath—
she can hear them hiss—then shear
like mortars exploding sexual shrapnel
through each body in the room.
Instructed by the singed fingers of dark angels, hope
marries fear, each note a prayer
and a summons,
a razor, a kiss
tipped in blood.

This is the house of music
speaking in the language of flames, house
going to ash but never destroyed, house
crackling and dying and whole.

Violinist, your prince is the molten center
of your own hunger's instrument.
Even roses lose their color
to the tintinnabulation
of Bach's last bars thrust across taut strings.

If whole notes could fly, these
would be cranes
                    made of iron and lace.

BLOOD FLOWER

If I were taken beyond the ocean, into Paradise and
forbidden to write, I would refuse the ocean and Paradise.

—Marina Tsvetayeva
Russian poet

Tonight I should be dancing with my best friend
in some monsoon-humid Tucson bar,
my hips swinging to memories old
as the diamond pictographs etched in stars,

but I cannot leave your poems. Their flint
blistering my hands. In photos, black as ice,
vast spruce forests stun your eyes
in the Siberia taiga Stalin banished you to.

Here, a cricket sings to desert
far from the sulfur racket grinding the city.
Was there a piano, at least,
a stray balalaika to buffer silence
        that tasted liked rusted tin
and roared like a wolverine so starved
it could not gnaw through grief's walls.

Not one friend came to break
through the mausoleum of your room.
Stalin stole every last ruble, denied you bread,
but the worst card of havoc he dealt
forbade you to write. You
        who called love, a flower watered with blood,
were finally abandoned by every lover.

Marina, the three syllables of your name knock
hollow as a necklace of crow bones.
I think of you alone except for poems scratched
on scraps you stuffed beneath your bed, verse
clandestine as passion burning the aging folds of your skin.

There wasn't even a river's brash current
to stir stallion memories stampeding your blood
until longing silted your veins, choked
the last images conjuring love
you could no longer compose.

How much poverty can any woman take—
your husband's chest shattered by a firing squad,
        just another enemy of the state,
one daughter starved in a Moscow orphanage,
another daughter and a beloved sister,
ash scattered in concentration camps?

With nothing left for your tongue
        but winter's awful ghost flowers, you refused
            the ocean, then paradise
                as you bent into the noose.

On TV, we cannot miss the way Stalin rhymes
with Putin as he flexes bare biceps
cradling tiger cubs on his lap. Which poet
will he murder next?

I would give you tonight, Marina,
        your tree, a mountain ash, that
dances wild outside my door to wind
awakening beneath the healing wheel of stars.

GENESIS REVISITED: THE CHERNOBYL BUFFALO

for Mary McGarvey and the buffalo

*Some 150,000 square kilometers in Belarus, Russia and Ukraine are
contaminated and stretch northward of the nuclear plant site as far as 500
kilometers. An area spanning around the plant considered "the exclusion zone"
is essentially uninhabited.*

You would see dystopia come true as your skin, if you could walk
these glowing forests growing up
through pavement in the abandoned city. Mushrooms
crack sidewalks, vines and bushes
chink condo walls while bourgeois houses sink like stumps
into a wilderness that would excite Thoreau or Muir
as much as frighten the ghosts of my greatgrandparents
irradiated in the path of the fallout.

Through the girdered skeleton of the nuclear plant
is a perfect view of the rotting skyline and,
restored by once-extinct beavers,
the labyrinthine channels of the Pripyat Swamp that stopped
even Genghis Khan's bloody march.

Now, a few researchers are allowed to roam The Exclusion Zone,
hefting Geiger Counters that click like an explosion of typewriters
tapping obituaries for buffalo bones, tree limbs,
phosphorescent soil. But, what they discover is destruction
that begets Eden complete with angels—
healthy packs of gray wolves, buffalo,
moose, sturdy deer herds,

white-tailed eagles, ravens, and miraculous
reincarnated beavers—pristine beyond their scientific dreams.

Against toxic apartment walls, crumbling schools,
an echoing hospital, wolves curl
against howling winter snows.   Come spring, buffalo
graze at ease between sprouting deciduous trees
that were once shopping malls.

How many decades have we feared apocalypse
born from splitting atoms to incinerate our enemies?
Who thought we could play tag with the sun and win?
It's no secret that the self-destruction we craft is
precisely what this planet needs to heal, to spawn
ozone we continue to deplete, clean up multitudes
of poisons we've shit all over our gifts.

Think of it all restored—the smooth lope
of wolves over clean snow, buffalo
and their spiritual eyes we exterminated world-wide,
the wide leaves of rainforest trees spreading
instead of urban sprawl, generating what
we could breathe deep to live,
what we tried to kill, divine.

The Trick

Who, if I cried out, would hear me among the angels'
hierarchies? And even if one of them suddenly
pressed me against his heart, I would perish
in the embrace of his stronger existence.

—R.M. Rilke

Never think that war, no matter how necessary,
nor how justified, is not a crime.

—Ernest Hemingway

LONG DISTANCE HOME

In your album tattooed
with Army Air Corps patches,
the women in tinted photos
were dark and naked

and wore their hair frizzed
wild as a wolf pup's fur.
They held amazed piglets
to their breasts that stretched

swollen as zucchini to their waists
astounding our eyes and tongues
that formed the demeaning nickname:
Fuzzy Wuzzies.

Slouched in wrinkled uniform,
you stared from pictures, Father,
framed by jungle, centered
in your cocky smile.

In others, you sprawled like a child
at play behind the machine gun,
wire-rimmed glasses
mirroring vine light.   You

told us you were lost,
forgotten on New Guinea for two years
and made gold jewelry to forget
the jungle rot in your knee,

the man who committed suicide
in your tent, the way your spine
cramped, bent around guns
in tails of B-25s during battles

we had to memorize in school.
In Italy, you grew so tired of repeating
destructions's crazy names, you screamed
as you pounded the floor of your plane: *Sweat and Pray.*

Now, half a continent away,
your voice hollows, recalling
the lonesome frenzy of birds
lifting strafed wings over a jungle at dusk.

In my kitchen on Discovery Bay,
across remembered halftones of light,
I hear your voice warm as whiskey.

THE TRICK

for my brother, John Uschuk

I

Drifting from houselights, dogs
whose eyes flare like searchlights
cross the broken dark.   Sophisticates of alleys,
warriors to cat-calling cats
they ignore seasonal lights
caroling from windows as they hunt shadows
under Arcturus's icy eye,
guardian bear who circles packs.

Scenting spores, the dogs scout blind ground.
Snow smothers their footfalls.
They listen for the one give-away sound,
the stroke of breath or stray hand
against fabric, betraying
ambush, a sudden night attack.

II

Hellgate wind is the backward wind
that rockets from the East strafing the valley.
No cloth can stop this immodest surveyor of flesh
as it snaps canyon rock, quick-freezes bone,
ignites sleeping roofs with the blue afterburn of snow.

I cannot sleep but wonder
what I am mate to in all this ice, what
sudden break in temperature fuels my blood?

III

The dogs mock-battle, crisscross fox and goose
through the unbearable perfection of powder.
This is the child's game we loved—our boots
the first to scuffle graffiti into the fresh fall.

> *The trick to survive miring drifts*
> *is to outrun the pack,*
> *perfect snarls,*
> > *then bite.*

Beneath snow drifts packed ten feet deep, we
dug tunnels, hollowed out
wolf dens winding blue as winter sun.
In imaginary wars, we stalked invisible enemies
or were killed, then rose
laughing to die again.
We strapped on Dad's old helmets,
the World War II mess kit
he etched with silver palm trees.
In the long deep cold we lost his medals—
        Oak Leaf Clusters, striped campaign ribbons,
the Bronze Star—everything but his stories
and those bullets of his imperfect metamorphosis that
slammed into our home.

IV

My brother, in those rainbright days
when blood showered like pennies around you, and
sense leaked from the world
        like helium from a foil balloon,
I couldn't see your hands at war in Vietnam.

TV bombarded us with the severed
limbs of charred children,
napalm-snuffed villages, a whole
country disemboweled every night at dinner.
You wrote me that you stood
on top of an ambulance while mortars
tore wounds in the green earth,
and you couldn't stop anyone's screams.

So far from answers, I mailed cookies,
chocolate and poems, but
I couldn't send you snow banks
or the way to come home.
Even now, white phosphorus blinds your dreams
and your buddy, decapitated
in the first battle, still
throws his head through your heart.

V

There are no dens I can dig for you.
I move from open night through
rooms glowing with asphyxiated light.
My shadow is snail white and
clings to the wall I fail to break.

Lost to insistent wind, barking circles
this town. I am more awake
than I ever need to be,
listening to storms assault mountains
older than any of our names
for war or peace.

If you were here now, I'd point out Arcturus,
steady and iridescent between
threatening clouds, star bear who guards
unmoved by Hellgate cold.

What can melt all this ice?
For you, a charm of snow and wind
to scour from your nights
the blood-bite of your dreams.

KNOWING THE ENEMY

This is the house of my enemy
constructed from the honeycombed vertebrae
of my spine, house where I snap on lights
to navigate the leafed labyrinth of my enemy's desire.

These are the riddled hands of my enemy
yanking the pin from a phosphorous grenade
to toss into the nest of questions
distressing my rebellious heart.

These are the eyes of my enemy
nearsighted as my own, lids thin as caddis wings,
opening on the shadows of deer sliding like messages
from the dead through pines outside our doors.

These are the pelvic bones of my enemy
glowing alive with my blood, aching from cold stars
tattooing the uniforms of generals issuing orders
as I squat behind an exploded Humvee in Kabul.

These are the thighs of my enemy
smeared with the same wet earth as mine,
tangling sweating sheets, unhoused
by bullets fired into the unarmed students we've become.

This is the brain of my enemy
ticking with plans for peace, lifted
on hope's deceptive wings flapping
dark feathers just out of our reach.

This is the tongue of my enemy,
inarticulate with passion, slurring the crisp syllables
of my language as it learns the triggers
and skrees of love's hunting songs.

This is the heart of my enemy,
knocking out my ribs as dawn bruises
sky's intent, drum of fortune beating against
the vast loneliness of unknowing we've frantically built.

FERRY SHELLING

You hear the rubber bladder bleat before
you see geese, heavy-bodied
stroking their way south
this season of rain ferries cut through
on their daily runs to the San Juan Islands.
From the Narrows Bridge, I trace
the long wake of the Fox Island Ferry
as it navigates whirlpools, the churn
and balk of contrary currents.

Over radio, the newscaster's voice is
gentle as Pacific fog, recounting
how yesterday an unarmed ferry bound for Lebanon
was blasted by a Syrian gunboat.

You hear shells before you see them—
a whoompf like an indignant sigh, then
the whistle in your gut
before the detonation murders the near world.

The report relays only six killed, all
anonymous slaughter
except the twenty-six year old man
returning from Cyprus with tickets for Canada
and a new life, to take his pregnant wife
away from Beirut's daily ecumenical argument
of mortars and car bomb fires.

Did the young man see it all
in a flash of phosphorus
before the concussion stilled everything?

His wife inconsolable in black veils, wailing
over his plain coffin
bought with refunded airline tickets?
His son, a fetal fist of revenge
already uniformed and clutching
the updated Uzi
floating in blood inside the tense womb?

How will his son fill his grave?
Did gore and pain finally create
numinous prophecy?
Or is life no metaphor, just
what it seems—today, what was young
and pregnant with the foxfire of hope
is forgotten by the traffic of the world.
Around the globe, grief shouts
but desolation is such a quiet creature.

Driving across the bridge intersecting
the wake of the Fox Island Ferry,
most of us will register the news
as a slight gust of helplessness
rustling through our memories.
Perhaps we won't hear at all how silent
the space where water and air meet
or how infinite the silver wake
stained by sunset,
                    this brushstroke of blood
that seems to lead to the end of the world.

HOROSCOPE

for Rick and Terry

In my hand, the bird of fear twists its beak to read
the horoscope that predicts its own conquest,
fear that scrapes the gut raw as green curry, fear
caught in the shear winds of torture, capsizing
places like Myanmar where hundreds of unarmed monks
are shot or beaten until their flesh is the ripped
color of sacred robes saturating capitol streets.

Take Venus, blood diamond that rises
over sun's death. What does it regret?
Thousands of nerves frizz, go numb
with nothing left to say when knuckles
splinter on cheek bones or labia
are hot-wired to Delco batteries
in the heart's interrogation chambers.

Last month the surgeon stripped
my brother's esophagus, that chemo-frayed ribbon, from
his chest, pulled up his stomach
like a tender purse, sewed it
to the end of his throat. Vietnam combat Vet
drenched again and again in Agent Orange,
he grew lumps that shaped themselves to one
tumor, a topographical map of fear,
with hooked fingers squeezing
off what he would eat to survive.

In my lifeline, there has never been a year
without war's acetylene scorching
tongues from young mothers, strapping
plastic explosives to its teenage chest
assured of a righteous recliner in heaven, flensing
strips of flesh from children to sell
in tyranny's global convenience stores.

Between the Mound of Jupiter and red
Saturn, I'd draw deeper my heart line
to ferry those Congolese boy-soldiers
hopped up on amphetamines, hefting M16s
taller than their twelve year old spines
before they can massacre more village girls
at whom, in other lives, they
might begin to wink.

On Arrowhead Mountain, we measure the size
of a puma's prints in spring mud, crossing
elk and deer tracks, kicking up
soggy moss as it sprang. From its mangled
winter nest, unvanquished,
illiterate,
the bird of fear still wails.

RUINED HONEY

Blurry via satellite, tonight,
a woman runs with her baby across
Hamra Street. Her back, machine-gunned,
stains with orange-sized wounds.
She jerks in yellow dust.
What is not seen is that
those slugs draw a skewer of blood
between mother and child.
What is not seen is
that morning, the woman heard her baby
laugh, dipped her forefinger in honey, then
rubbed her child's lips
to make laughter come again.

On the evening news, Israeli bombs
slam Bierut's ashes into the sea.
        The camera holds the stunned faces
of girls who are burst
by mortar fire, then
fire.

It's a short news clip
among many we're lost to.
What we cannot know is that these girls—
who would learn to smoke cigarettes in another country,
        or, who in America, might play
baseball in designer jeans—
                these girls may have stopped
to flirt with a jewelry vendor

when above the silver jangling, they heard
the whoomph, crack and boom
of artillery exploding their homes on the next street.

Maybe, they thought they were lost,
their dozing street transformed
into a terrified landscape
of smoking bricks and bodies;
thought they were lost
until they saw the neighbor with her baby
run toward them, warning them
through the rising dust.

The clip is distant and deceptive as a war movie,
but if once we'd seen
those dark women brew white coffee
from orange blossoms
perhaps saving some petals to crush
like perfume into their skins
waiting to be loved, then might those bullets
shatter our hearts,
                    then might their burning daughters
and blasted sons shock us,
shock us like honey suddenly
ruined on a baby's lips.

WHITE PHOSPHORUS AFTER HANUKKAH

From the stench of her wounds,
still burning the hospital bed, swaddled
in agonized air, this woman's grief
scalds like the specter of her daughter
when the missile hit, splitting
her kitchen and incinerating her baby
in her arms. Her daughter vaporized
as she watched. Smoke
wreathes her arms, her chest
that continue to char
just as the burn of her memory
still sears deep screams, hers,
her daughter's, blurred with
the reptilian hiss of Israeli missiles
sizzling to Gaza, tracing beautiful arcs
to her kitchen.
What god
or monster could imagine this?

Even students know white phosphorus
broils under water, boils
in tissues so deep they no longer resemble
anything so much as cooked goat.
What seven bright angels
of hope can call this the Promised Land?

A nurse wraps this woman's arms in yellow
salve, kisses her forehead
with cucumber's cool lips. Her daughter

rises from ash, carries the baby
into her mother's room.
Take it all back,
she sings. *Take it back. Back.*
Take it back before Hanukkah
and its deadly Festival of lights.

ERASING THE NAMES

News reports sprout bouquets of pain—
car bombs, suicide bombs, bombs pasted
to mosque doors, duct taped
to the ribs of a teen stepping up onto a bus
loaded with workers in Tel Aviv.
Bombs shred worshippers and ambassadors alike,
rip open mothers and six-year-old girls,
nephews and grandfathers, distilling
unidentified char from
human beings and their tears,
from the laughter of the loved, the spiteful tongue,
sweat rivering the skin of passion,
eyes unscarred by fear.
                                          Bombs
without names bent on erasing names,
bombs crammed with nails polished by hate,
screeching the sacred tongues of revenge,
ticking with the clocks of heaven for martyrs
wound by dark-eyed virgins,
bombs riveted with economic lies
and political advantage, bombs
without ears to hear the screams from maimed lips,
bombs without eyes to see the way
survivors bend to kiss blood from pavement,
bombs without hands to caress
despised skin, bombs
without hearts to forgive
to forgive
to forgive.

REMEMBERING THE TET OFFENSIVE AS
TROOPS SHIP OUT FOR A U.S. ATTACK ON IRAQ

for Roger C. Frank

A fighter jet etches ink white as sperm
on the stark sky while January troops deploy
from Camp LeJeune, just like my first husband
did in 1968 on his way to Viet Nam
to wipe the Commie Gooks off the map.
Before he could spell Khe Sahn, think
massacre, he was machine-gunned
then bayoneted, left to die two days
in a jungle valley of shimmering green bamboo
near the clear stream he couldn't reach
before the chop chop of the Medevac arrived.
One of three survivors of a whole company
of young marines slaughtered, he wanted to toss
the Purple Heart in the trash.
I remember during the long Michigan winter
his night sweats, the way
he'd shout the apartment walls awake, shake
to the screams of his buddies as they choked
on their own blood, clotted by indifferent flies,
some disemboweled, legs,
arms, faces cratered as frosted poppies.
He'd point to the mean hieroglyphs of red scars,
a pinched cummerbund of bullet
and stab wounds cinching his waist,
then ask me, new bride, too young
to be a Sphinx, the riddle I couldn't reason out.

What was this for? What for?
as he headed to the kitchen for anesthetic beer,
the amber mattress of whiskey straight.
In three years he joined his company underground.

He was handsome, gung-ho like these teen soldiers
interviewed on CNN, cocky
as oiled M16s, proclaiming
their belief as each generation before them
that they will fight the war to end all wars.
Behind them, wives and girlfriends wave
small American flags that break
in the brittle wind.

SPOTTING WHOOPERS

For Don and Lynn Watt

Swallowing dread, we drive to the Texas coast
where sun tosses white grenades of light
bursting cumulous banks. None of us
have given up on this dispirited world, look
for signs to reverse blood curses.

Salt-balmy this air I'd send
to my nephew and Don's son deploying
to Iraq this month of kites and wind-bag politicians
staying a course set on greed.

Pulling into Aransas Refuge, we thrill
to possibility, to see those rarest of cranes, our chances
as slim as this trip to the edge of our nation
on a day shiny as a foil birthday balloon, as fragile.

Up ramps umbrelled by new oak leaves,
we climb breathing humidity and pollen
to the viewing platform. Through
my binocular lenses swims first
a huge brown sow with her litter
across a channel, then a miraculous curve
of feathers, luminous as polar ice,
above knobby knees high-
stepping into swamp grass, where
tea-colored Gulf waves froth
over the small clatter of blue crabs,

across sand spits, gorse and lacy wild daisies
intersecting the tracks of raccoons,
roseate spoonbills, and deer.

We are lucky. Whoopers seem to materialize
Just for us. Bright as arctic wind, they bend
intent on their hunt until we lose sight
of their red-gashed heads, lush eye-liner
dramatic as a pharoh's kholl, snowy primaries
dipped in ink. Joy-spun
by beauty, by these birds, celestial
and dancing on the edge of destruction,
our words fail, just as they have failed
to stop war's unappeasable appetite.

Oh, prayer beads of fortune, safely
lift these cranes into the salty cradle of blue Gulf air
that mimics air above a gulf a half a world away
where my nephew will fly to a war
like ice to fire
leaving us behind who have not learned
the charm to turn roadside mines into love notes,
who too often keen the stiletto syllables of loss,
whose nightmares are lit by mortar fire and IEDs
who cannot find any real map for peace.

Tonight the moon opens its white jaws and howls.
It has no need of patriotic slogans or sacrifice.
Defying extinction, cranes snap up blue crabs
in their anthracite beaks, then
roost in branches heaving reflected light.

PARACHUTE

Before he shipped out of Italy, my Air Corps dad
hired a seamstress to stitch
a scarf from his silk parachute
not for a girlfriend, but for his mom
waiting in Michigan for him to come home.

Tail-gunner, his six-foot frame bent
a boney comma around the machine gun in a B 29—
on missions that dropped thousand pound bombs
to demolish towns in the Italian Alps,
Yugoslavia and Germany.

What good was a parachute? he asked,
telling about the afternoon
his plane, *Sweat and Pray*, flew formation,
on a bombing raid, in the box,
above the aluminum glint of snow
dividing granite slopes where Eidelweiss bloomed.

Just as he waved to his buddy, a gunner
who flashed thumbs up in the next plane,
it exploded, his face incinerating
the sky, then a lightning storm of flak
chinked and popped through the tail where he sat.

My dad hit the deck, smashed fists
that had won the Golden Gloves
against the frozen sheet metal floor,
Jesus Christ, what am I

doing here? Jesus Christ Almighty.
When his plane skidded in on its belly, mechanics
counted a hundred holes in the tail alone,
No way you could have been in this
and not been hamburger. No way.

Fingering campaign medals,
my dad looked through me with eyes
liquid as the blue air above peaks.
That's why they send boys to war. No
grown man would go.

Now in the next century, I unfold
his parachute, watching fighter jets
scream to the Persian Gulf and yet another enemy.

I read the dead names screened in silk—
12th Airforce. Hoo Doo Hawk.
Red the Wrecker. Lady from Hades. Ace of Pearls.
Nightmare. And I cannot sleep.

EUCARIST

Sky is a delphinium the full moon planted blind in the blue sway
its petals spread wide across memory. Easter
and I recall the acrid taste of fried boiled eggs
I loved on my tongue, crisp eucharist of my father's laughter,
fried dyed eggs our ritual this one day a year
my agnostic father fed us and we almost believed
in an end to his machine gun anger, curses
shot like flack into our fear, the quick regret
of his Russian bear arms as he hugged us to sleep.

When he died the day after Mom's birthday, we piled
his favorite Snickers bars, his Bronze Oak Leaves,
his silver Air Corps wings and fists full of medals
atop his corpse that could have broken
into laughs or tears at any second.

Today, I believe in ice thinning
along the runs of Vallecito Creek, the way
the molten glass green current storms
to take boulders, our longing hearts.
Water's ovation drowns out every sound
but its own freight train lyrics
lifting deadfall pines bigger than my car
and swirling frostbite at my resurrected feet.

Two pair of ospreys wheeze the language of clouds
to one another as they talon trout from the reservoir to feed
wobbly hatchlings in their twig-knit nests.

I can almost hear my father's yard swing
creak to a halt as he holds his massive arm
still on its back, so that the robin
he talks to and feeds, hops atop his bicep finally at rest.

OPERATION IRAQI FREEDOM ENDS

A bluebird slips between electric wires
and I remember waking to the radio static of the Vice President
saying there was no choice but war,
but there were no plans for war, a confabulation
confusing as the tongue of a captive raven, split
so he'll talk to amuse the neighbor
who nursed the raven back to health
after it was hit by a car in the street
and now keeps it caged in a backyard
where it has learned the price of being saved.

TOURING TEREZIN

for Naomi Benaron and Marilyn Kallet

I

In the high barred windows, hosts of swallows nest
in the ghost uniforms of Gestapo
who interrogated Jews in transit to Dachau,
Auschwitz or Treblinka. Interrogated
is such a civil verb; these impenetrable syllables
replicate the watery clatter of barley
or wheat in wind, not bruised optic nerves,
split lips or kicked testicles of those without answers.

Barn swallows swallows blue as Czech streams raise
chicks frantic for food while tourists snap pictures of rust-eaten sinks,
cracked mirrors, rows and rows of splintery beds
knocked together from warped planks.

Sixty years later, there is no indifference large enough
to mute the screams of children ripped like petals
from fathers and mothers, no eyemasks to blind
the old spirits holding out the slaved femurs of children
like offerings to this green amnesiac countryside.

Between headstones, roses bloom almost obscene,
red as lipstick or fresh bullet wounds
stitching the torsos of the too-young herded to the grassy hillock
then thrown into pits at this model camp.

In these barracks we can still hear children
who painted pictures black with war,

who practiced a cheerful play for Nazi cameramen
while interrogators caved in their parents' chests.
How can we escape the flutter of all those wings—
out of thousands crammed on winter trains,
less than a hundred adults, only one tenth of the children,
moth-thin in nightmare's high wind, survived.

Did they, too, believe that birds are the spirits of ancestors?
Silence drives our tourist bus home. We watch swallows
along the road build mud nurseries
tucked in the steel beams of a bridge,
far from human reach.

VETERANS DAY

In the cemetery, yellow ginko leaves
waxy as embalmed fans warm grave stones
arranged on an abacus clicking granite beads
that name the dead.
                              Under an oak, a young
woman kicks through autumn to a flag
marking the stone she bends to clean,
chucking a hemlock branch, bare palms
brushing debris from the brass name plate,
where her veteran lies; whether father,
brother, husband or lover, she cries.
                                        My lost soldiers
are ash. Father. Brother. Husband. Their stories circle
like crows, cawing machine gun rounds
or pop like the single-shot from a 45 that bloodied
my father's tent when his friend
blasted his teeth into his brain, writing
his own discharge papers from war.

I remember a letter from Viet Nam,
my brother wrote in sprials on a medal of honor
certificate, asking me to tell the press
about him on patrol in Laos, torching
villages, killing Laotians, contradicting
the army's official reports. Each life
he snuffed, a notch flensed from his future joy.

Yesterday, over coffee, a young teacher
asked my advice. Her student,
an Afghanistan war vet, scares her
with his stories, a wedding party
shredded by phospohorus rockets that missed
the Taliban terror cell.
                           What can I teach
her about night terrors, trip-wire
nerves, ground teeth, the reflex
to pull the trigger?   In this graveyard, I read
the names killed in WW I and II, Korea,
Viet Nam, Iraq.
                           I want their last
stories to scratch through raw earth,
through the lucent satin sheen
of ginko leaves, screaming each lost dream,
lost love, exploded gut, eye
gouge, multiple-amputee,
oozing strafe wounds, brain bruise,
if that's what it takes
to bring those who will next be veterans
home, never to send them again
to fight for freedom that is no more
than a word on a tomb.

Talk About
Your Bad Girls

For one human being to love another:
that is the most diffuclt of all our tasks,
the ultimate, the last test of proof,
the work for which all other work
is but preparation.

—R.M. Rilke

may the tide
that is entering even now
the lip of our understanding
carry you out
 beyond the face of fear
may you kiss
the wind then turn from it certain that it will
love your back

—Lucille Clifton

The real revolution is love.

—Joy Harjo

AFTER READING
LOUISE BOGAN'S JOURNALS

Outside on this floodplain subdivision, the hiss
of irrigation hoses disturbs day and night.
Theirs is an awful breathing,
the monotonous whisper of locusts.
Relentless witness,
ubiquitous desire,
it is the sound of water that soothes and erodes.

What peril life places us in
When love fails the heart. The heart,
the watershed of the mind.
What peril when the flume claims us
and we become the woman
whose hand rakes the parlor wall
to stop the flowing
so we sink into water so transparent
we see no arm above ours,
no lips saying no.

There rises in each of us a mad woman as afraid of water
as of losing love.
She cries when we walk into surf,
wounds us beside rivers
whose currents could cleanse our tears.
She is what we always hear
listening to the sad frenzy of tides.
What could drown us we drink to live.

I won't say I know
how it was for you, just as
I can't reproduce in my garden
the exact red-rimmed yellow eye
of the marigold that caught yours
in your mother's hospital room.
It silenced all the roses
just as the crash of the mill flume
deafened you each time your love fled.

During breakdowns you refused
the awful anxiety of roses that friends brought,
their red petals fussy drawing rooms
you could never enter.

Water was aluminum in the painful pitcher
beside your bed, keeping you awake
with its thin waves
washing against unyielding shores.
Giving up the fickle husband
who broke your dreams, you gave yourself
to words that emptied around you
when the last attack came.
They echo still.

I would have told you then
that it is water that carrries you,
that finally, water
forgives the heart.

THERE ARE NO IN-LAWS
IN THIS POEM

For Emilia Phillips

All the chests of blue horses
muscle mountain dawn to rain
as I open an email from a friend sneezing
among Bradford pear and redbud blooms.

      Her poem rings a small bronze bell of longing
in the glazed eye of a kitten her aging dog
killed in her yard. New bride riding wild
her own carousel of desire
past sentiment or need, she catalogues what's lost
washed up on the shore of her verse.

      There is no loneliness as complete
as those memories that leave bones
in the path of the everyday for us to trip on
just when we think we understand
the multiple personalities of love in a handful of clover.

      A thousand penguins are found
dead on the shores of Southern Chile. Mysterious,
scientists say, none tangled in fishing nets nor poisoned, no
mass suicide. Seven more penguin species
list endangered in December as
Antarctic ice continued its slide to rising seas.

      Walking red sandstone
outside Monument Valley with my love, we unearthed
a human jaw bone complete with three teeth.

No flesh or hair clung to its fossil shape.
Turning it like a Tarot card in my hand, we left
the jaw to the fortunes of wind, fate nestled by warm rock.

        Outside the morning window, small as your chin,
mountain chickadees dare the blue thrash of magpies,
the death-white eyes of Steller's jays.   I
am cheered by their wheeze in the piñons,
the way their asthmatic laughter finds splinters of light
despite storms blowing up thunder from a horizon obscured.

BANKING THE FIRE

for Jack Heflin and Walter Pavlich

Like midnight all of it came true,
the leaded glass doors tattooing rainbows to early snow,
a closed casket,
the windless flag,
the mourner on crutches who shook my hand.
Three nights running
the same dream,
the funeral of a friend whose face I couldn't see.

Insomniac as new pine snapping
against premature cold, I stared
at sky and listened to
its cross rhyme of loneliness and fear.
Banking the fire, I almost refused
to answer the phone blasting news—
how the suicide bullet traced
a blue path of release through John's brain.
For weeks he swore he saw God expand
like hydrogen gas inside his camera lens.
And the too bright light.
Finding him three days dead, his mother
said that Mozart played again and again
on his stereo to no one but snow.

Like silhouettes behind frosted glass,
messages are never clear. Take
the single time I saw a daylight meteor
arc an orange brow across the acetylene eye of the sky.

A coincidence, some claimed, that earlier
that afternoon the local clairvoyant died
from the sudden failure of her heart.

II

Now this move back to the Bitterroots
after three years living with desert's signs.
How glad we are to be loved
in the house of friends, sharing dreams
beyond the power of wounds we endure.

From the porch we trace the flight of ravens
sure on morning updrafts, the sway
of Pasque flowers resurrecting the woods,
the lure of Balsam root's bright yellow skirts,
and it is good to see snow shrink under the trees,
to unbutton our flannel shirts.
Winter was easy now that trilliums split
the dead quilt of leaves. Perhaps
this is all we need to understand.

Walter, you tell us that your grandfather comes to you
as a raven, and you can't decipher his dark tongue.
We can splice the spiral lattice of genes
easy as speaker wires, but how
can we learn to live with our dead?

Morning coffee gone, we turn
to the amnesia of routine.
I remember John, how convinced he was
that love would prevail

even though he feared his own delicate hands.
Splitting ripe chunks of fir for the fire
we'll bank tonight, we share the center of this season
so old it needs no maps
to chart the wild meteorology of the heart.

RAFTING THE GORGE
EATEN BY WHITE WATER

for Bill and Happy

> *So, the world happens twice —*
> *once what we see it as;*
> *second it legends itself*
> *deep, the way it is.*

—William Stafford

I

We climb the steady trail
above iced runoff abusing the gorge
cut by Vallecito Creek, flanked
by the sweet reek of wild geranium
and tiny white shooting stars.
Pine pollen turns the wind as we turn
to each other, giddy
to escape computers, cell phones,
all bad news that would find us.

Three decades now we've been lover-friends
snickering at the twitch of chipmunks
cheeping from forest floors, fresh steam
from bear shit, inhaling wildflowers
and the musk of winter-mashed leaves, then arguing
over stupid things the way lodge pole pines
grind against each other in storms
they soon forget. Nearly noon and
we adore sky's wide intuition
that hikes us back to our right minds.

II

Like some bear sharing a fat salmon
you've swatted ashore, you relay
your morning's info read, that
in some women, dentata are real,
along vaginal lips, cysts
line up, and, in each cyst, a small tooth.
Here, in the Weminuche Wilderness, truth is granite
cracked by sub-zero winds, smooth
rock bellies tattooed by lime green lichen,
round as open mouths.
Here, among these rocks, I vow not to bite.

III

We stop to scan each snow-striped ridge,
while a thousand feet below us
ravens and finches flit over the insatiable appetite
of white water bashing boulders
in a perpetual multi-truck wreck
roaring at the bottom of the canyon we descend.

New Solomon's seals unfurl
elegant leaves so full of shine, they gleam
like oiled green silk I stop to stroke before we grab
the cutting edge of stone, slim hawthorne twigs
to slow our slide down the steep slope to the creek.

I sit streamside awash in a sudden hatch
of butterflies, blue as propane flames, fragile
in their maiden voyages across the vast current.
Astonishing, their wings fit exactly over my lids. They lift
criss-crossing with ease what could drown us.

IV

You walk upstream, the white wolf
leashed to your wrist, jumping logs jammed
in boulders, deftly leaping from
bark to waveslick rock skirting the deep chop
deafening us to raven croak, each
other's shouts of wonder. Above your hat
disappearing behind a huge boulder, sky's impossible
blue catches a dragonfly's solitary wings
while a cold gust from Granite Peak riles needles,
spikes wild cherry leaves. Sometimes,
it seems too lovely to be alive.

What has fate stashed up its faded sleeve?
You snap photos of runnels from melting ice, clarified
as the aquamarine eye of a mountain lion, out
of any human control, this beauty
turning sorrow over in its clear hands, is
terrifying as the sudden deaths of those we love,
increasing with each passing year, until
the fatal current restores to us possibility.
Both sides of the blade glitter, slice deep.

We ration what's left of dried berries,
haul ourselves over windfall trees,
through wild briars, up granite's sharp shanks,
grateful to breathe the icy creek, to
hear the dogs growldance ahead,
to trust our legs, once again, to carry us
the bone-aching miles home.

FIRE SONG

for Juanita Melendez and Joy Harjo

I sing sweet nothings to the orange mouths of hyssop,
red penstemon, grace notes I plant
despite our decade long drought.
When has soil endured such thirst?

All my weight jumped onto the shovel
drives the blade just an inch
into concretized ground, the way it must have
when the ancient ones left kivas to bake in relentless sun.

Women are hummingbirds who need
the passionate smear of red to sustain them,
moisture to soothe chapped knuckles, to plump
crow's feet stretched from eyes and lips.

My friend's in love, heat rising
through the green branches of her longing.
I am a nun in my garden, dreaming rain
to pound into earth's cracked and neglected hips.

I feel sorry for the trees, spray piñon and juniper
needles so dry they snap when I squeeze them.
I read that, in Sudan, where women are stoned
to death, drought widens its clipped grin.

I finger beaded earrings my friend sent
the blue of ocean, lapis lazuli wings,
forget-me-nots blooming beside Lime Creek

runoff high in the Rockies that have
at Solstice already lost their snowpack.

Across the San Juan Mountains, smoke
wags its silver fox tail, smothers our valley.
Pyroclastic clouds burst to the stratosphere of our fear
that everything will burn when the Western horizon explodes.

Before sunset, we drive to the wolf refuge
where eighty wolves pace, nerves clicking
from wood smoke choking their enclosures.
Jewelers, Juanita and I wire dog carriers, test the strength
of mesh doors. Set free, the wolves will surely be shot.

Ranchers forget wolves are sacred on Ute land, aim
at them as they do all ghosts they fail to understand,
down the blue barrels of their ignorance.

Flames lick the river, gauge how far to leap
to gorge on crackling sage, bear grass,
rabbit bush so dry a small woman can crush it
to powder across her own life line.

Working to save the wolves, we brush past cornflowers,
periwinkle blue, numinous as river mist at dawn.
There are ways of loving that howl at the moon of our need
and don't involve singing the blues.

In our last big fire, over 85,000 acres burned
the entire summer. Firefighters reported bears
coming up to them, standing on two legs,
holding up their burning paws, crying.

Ravens flying from flames, dropped
to earth, their lungs burst from pyroclastic heat.

Discussing Eros, a friend tells me that craving is addiction
that leads to destruction. Even mares crave rain.

In the Sudan, drought carves women
and children into thin twisted walking sticks.
Perfidious, the fire blows away from the wolves, spins
its smoke suddenly north. We continue to believe
in signs. Walking back to the car, Juanita
finds a stone in the shape of a heart. In my path,
an eagle wing feather, obsidian, flight edge soft as ash.

JUNE'S HOTTEST DAY
for Ella Uschuk

sweats through the armpits of Michigan's humid blue housedress,
     and my mother screams
          NOW!   George, it's time
                   her mouth a swollen peony, red
as the light that broils through her belly
where I twirl in my first waltz,
center of a blood apple, bulbous forehead
cocked earthward to chart the map of appearances.

Little vampire bat slick as a new leaf,
I would lick up the insects of fear
my mother will spend her life shrinking from.
The music I hear is water's promise
gushing to the linoleum floor,
the memory of red ocean,
the arterial blood of sky I will adore.

Oh, the delivery is white as hyped moonlight
spiked from ice that kills the senses, from
the rote logic of the surgeon's hands
who invents the name episiotomy.
Even safe, my underwater eyes
see the future of edges, the way
my mother must be cut to set me free.

Her veins screech across my brow, gushing
spasms pushing me from slow orbit,
and I am sucked forth, pulsing
through the nimbus of her swift contractions.

The doctor taps the cervical tympanum
unclenching my fontanel, and she names me
jesuschrist oh, shit!

Head first I dive as I will dive
all my life from her blood's worried embrace
to harsh white shadows that scour my face,
an emotional globe unflattening, lungs
ballooning to scream against strange hands
that begin to measure me, hanging me
        by my heels to see
the world's upside-down surgery.

A DREAM, MY CHILD

When in the thrift store
I found that child's satin dress,
its miniature sleeves opening the air
like lilac scent, I thought
of you who so often in dreams
swim in a quick release
of dark water from my inner thighs.
There is no pain, only a rush
rocking like a tide reversing.
Your head is slick with black hair
and you do not scream at displacement.

You have remained a dream, my child,
and as often as I have held you
nursing above the tightness
in my womb, I have awakened
startled but warm.
If there is anything I can tell you, now,
it is that I bought that dress, knowing
those folded wings may never open.
It lies with eyes shut
In violet light among my clothes.

My child, you have become
the words that breathe across
empty pages, an imperfection of longing
whose arrival is incredible.

TALK ABOUT YOUR BAD GIRLS

for Val

White water's our ritual, rafting
the Animas, river of lost souls,
run-off swollen, frothy as cappucino.
How do trout survive this torrent,
bashing metal sheets of water
that displace even boulders?
And us ridiculous in a rubber raft
that buckles and folds like a caterpillar
tossed from its safe limb by storm.

Talk about your bad girls. Fear
charges us. Not just
aluminum bullets of adrenaline stippling our tongues
nor the amphetamine rush of hormones,
        but the cold still idea of drowning.
Over-powered by the current's thrust
our muscles forget age and abuse, thrilled
tight as a dancer's belly.
When the raft pitches over rapids
we fly above its gunnels, cracking
our foreheads like rams, then
laugh at our survival
to sever long months of separation.

Summers of rivers tie us—
from the Umcompagre and the Blue,
to the industry-stunned Grand, to
the flat maligned Red Cedar

all the way back to the Lookingglass
with its pure amniotic flow through our girlhoods.

Remember the June we rafted the Platte
so lucid we could see
the lazy fanning of squaw fish over pebbles,
the drift of shadows ripple sand.
Looking up we caught the Goshawk
shocked up from the bloated steer, fly-blown
stink half-sunk in the trampled shore.

Weeks after, salmonella fevered your blood
and you couldn't sweat enough
death from your dreams.
We never imaginied clarity could be so final,
but that didn't keep you from next season's stream.
I wonder at those who risk it all—
the rock climbers, parachutists, deep
sea divers, tightrope walkers
and snake charmers of the world—what
offerings they make to manic gods.

All year you sculpt what you believe
while I image words.
                        Today we are tossed
like dolls in a vulnerable raft
on icy water that would forget us as soon as we fell in.
Our hands and feet are numb from it.
We'll survive this time. Summer
will shrink runoff from the trunks of pines.
The river's fatal rush binds us, beats
back awkward conversation
as we give over to this wilder sister
constantly churning on the edge of her song.

THE DEAD UNBURIED BY SPRING

Wind-ripped blonde, she died under a cedar tree, ancient
palomino, whose corpse I mistook for a drift
left by winter's last mountain blast.
Two years, we'd fed her windfall apples,
carrots, pears as we would a beloved
grandmother confined, wiping rheumy eyes,
patting atrophied flanks scarred by barbed wire,
astonished at her stamina to survive fate's micro bursts,
the brutal razor strap slaps of sub-zero cold.
She had no barn, but, at least, those who thought they owned her
did not shoot her or sell her for dog food.

What were the last things the mare saw
through those cataracts, smoky
as spring ice—astral
fire spit from a meteor etching desire
through the indigo sea
between Cassiopoeia and Orion
or the quick flick of a vole's tail
the exact shape of the new moon
on snow that piled against her knees?
Why do I imagine her death was born
at night? My only brother and father
left near midnight, decades and a continent
apart. How can I ever shake
the wet ash of their leaving from
grief's ulcerated cramping?

Now snow is wind's memory, tiny
magenta wildflowers spike up through marl
and sky frenzied by the jittery jazz of red-winged blackbirds.
Loss squeezes my torso in its blue arms.
The mare died alone under distant stars
the way my father and brother died alone, far
from those who raised them, who kissed their skin
alive, after sending us away whose love
would have moored them to earth longer than
their hearts could bear.

This bruised peach dawn
quick fires the mare's bleaching bones,
the disheveled rug of her hair
sinking into green that thickens
under cedars breathing this common air
the once-golden mare, my father
and brother have become.

FRENCH HORN

At twelve I loved the silvery bulge
of my horn's bell where fear
went mute as a scream
I polished with my sweater sleeve, then
clenched my lips
to high E loud enough
to squeeze anguish
into Bach's passion keen
as the erratic heartbeat of the wild kitten
I smuggled into my room.

Even now, I hear a French Horn
in my sleep, where no one
but the white blades of mountains
scrape my mother's tears
from my face.

       What was the shape
of her fear drifting blue as asphixiated lilies
or scratched as the old LPs
serving up Lady Day
or Bessie Smith
or Satchmo to the kitchen
where my mother
was always cold?

When she didn't see
me, I loved to watch her let down
her jaguar-colored pompadour.
No April downpour was
ever as dense as those tresses
she pinned up as she rocked
solitary as a birch
back and forth across
the gray linoleum
of her bottomless sorrow.

My mother could have
been a movie star, Merle Oberon
or Judy Garland, her
lips plump way before collagen,
her green eyes that flared like the multiple
depths of tides set on fire. Sometimes
my horn's wail could short circuit her nerves.
The time she threw off her clothes
and howled in the middle
of our dining room,
we all went deaf. So much of
her dance ended there that
I dropped out of orchestra, traded
my horn for a pen
I still tap to hear again
that sweet rhythm lost.

THORN OF DEVOTION

for Albert Kogel

I

Flying between Spanish swords, a merwoman
eludes scorpion bites, rattle snakes, all
toxins as she curls her clay tail
above buttocks scarred with iron oxide shields.
This sculpture smiles, her spiral
Aztec earrings repelling what wounds.

This noon yard doesn't sing, booms at
shrinking cactus, the boast from
bougainvillea's lewd lipstick leaves.
I wait in Albert's garden, a postmodern
rendering of heat waves, acrylic-drenched rags,
dog dishes, a dry fountain, aprons
smeared with his psyche's war paint.

Heat ticks on the patio, where I wait for my friend
to open the door to what only appears
to be locked, cavern of the fabulous
nailed together from broken dreams.

II

Panels line the walls, the first
inscribed with Sabe, she who knows,
Rez dog, split-eyed protector
who died two years and a lifetime ago.
Above her, mythic fish dive through blood orange

light, a sea composed wholly of sunset,
a way to say goodbye.
On my left, a burrowing owl terrifies us,
the dead stacked up in its coal black eyes, hunting .

In front of me, Sabe stands on her back legs.
She cannot die, beloved
figment, ghost eyes enlarged by joy.
Above her head floats a blue macaw
crowning her prophecy. Sabe multiplies
until she is Shiva dancing on each wall we face,
her life flame preserved, tongue
dripping with sweat and desire, her nose
so real it is cold. What fish feeds
her as she hums between two worlds?

Into tidal currents of carmine and blue, a woman
walks, black and white, her eye filling with loss,
with the knowledge that each loss plants
a new ocotillo, desert willow, all healing herbs.

There is something comforting in the way her neck
plants itself in the base of her skull, the way
her spine shimmers under her skin.
This, too, is knowing. Sabe gone to ash.
She who knows, preserved
in pigment, cannot die.

Like offerings, a trumpet and *Deux Cents Etudes Nouvelle*,
a French horn muted by saw dust, are laid
before the paintings. Here is the heart
of creation, where terror begins, juncture
of form and breath beyond words,
the unknowable alchemized

from doors we believe are locked.
Our hearts walk through the fish eye
magnifying death—keeps on walking
to break through the other side
only to return to this lived place.

III

What is a painter or a poet but a heart
that cannot stop walking, that creates
gold foil to wrap the sharpest thorn—
the thorn of devotion hooking the dog's eye,
a reef fish amused by the sea of its transformation,
the macaw blue as a hydrangea caught
in the screen door of its confusion.
Chopped into verse, severed as the soul,
what we make is music brushed with shifting
images carved from the inferno of need.

CRAFT LESSON

for Bryce Milligan

In his Victorian house, my friend hand-sews poems
into green paper covers embossed with a Celtic maze
while he watches Rachel Maddow
rage on TV against the latest atrocity, a truck driver
who opened fire at Fort Hood, just miles away
killing two fellow soldiers, wounding nineteen more.
No motive yet, they say. Even the lawn-sized flag
at the Ford dealership in San Antonio sags
slack-jawed at half mast, where NRA pro-guns buy
the latest in killer pickup trucks.

My friend's two children, one a poet,
another, a genius hooked on stars, read books
but call them clutter, shuttle them
out of their spare designer houses.
My friend will publish fourteen books this year, admits
ebooks support what he prints for love into pages.
His wife, a librarian, lifts blue light in her hands
illustrating the way her elementary students
read books on screens, might
never feel the heft and valleys of home-made paper.

A songwriter, my friend sews poems
into hand-made pages by the Texas State Laureate
about the triumph of song to lift the shamed boy
in all of us from our inability to pronounce
the enemy's language. His *yes, yes, yes* rattles
our brains from commercial sleep.

National news shows children from Guatemala
caged in dog pens along the border, waiting to be
deported, back to the gang violence they fled.
The camera pans one girl, four years old.
Where are you, Rachel Maddow, when
Congress turns its back on children?

In front of the Celtic harp his uncle bent
to beauty, my friend continues his craft.
This needle, too, moves the world.
What does a house without pages feel?
What Kevlar vest can it wear without words
to turn the bullets of the world
into songs to staunch its raging grief?

WHAT THE DEAD SPEAK

*for Anna Mashutina, playwright killed in a suicide bombing
in Domodedovo Airport in Moscow, January 25, 2011*

Did the flash come by gasp
or dream?
                    At 29 you blogged:
It seems to me that I have little time left.
Critics call your prose *"lacerating,"* where the alley cat
of *"the dehumanizing world reverses itself..."*
blows upside down, *"lands solidly on its feet."* Intuitive,
you always knew what language the dead speak.
Oh, *moya sestra Ukriane,* can the narrative
our bloody history ever clot and heal?

Your hand did not flip on the celebrity switch
when your plays won laurels, bowed instead
your lion colored head, embarrassed
by compliments, knowing
fame is a warped and tenuous stage, sets
stapled to fragile canvas, not nailed down.

Anna, you were afraid of flying. But, it wasn't
the creak of metal wings, an unstable fusilage
but the terminal shattering piped-in music,
cinderblock walls and terrorized flesh
that blew apart your future's plot.

Last night, a poet told me how she downs valium
before each flight so she won't feel the raw
yaw and bump of her flight terror. Bound

for home, her plane dropped and the businessman
next to her screamed so she kissed him, thrusting
her tongue into his fear. They kept kissing,
swollen mouths unhinged against
the dark hunger of annihilation they flew through
until the plane touched down. She said she could not
let go until she saw her new husband
waiting hot on the tarmac below.

Anna, you kissed no one but lacerating glass, never
retrieved baggage or ascended the dais
to accept your final prize.

What must have seared your husband's hand
as he punched again and again
your cell phone number? The policeman's words
burst shrapnel through the glass walls
of his heart. No firebird's blazing wings
or unfinished script, not even
            the eternal scream
of your three-year-old daughter
will ever resurrect what the world lost—
your slim feline body, the beautiful lazy eye, window
to your mind, brilliant, bone-splintered.

METEORIC

Neuropathy's ice blocks each step, just one
of chemo's aftershocks sizzling from my sole
to fingertips to my bald head, where
daily I try to reconfigure a path, the
exact trajectory back to human.

In Russia, my people, believing in beauty again,
rush to windows awed by a meteor's rare arc
burning a pure acetylene spine over snow
before the panes shattered, blasting glass
into their stunned familiar faces.
This is the rapture that wounds.

Take love and its singed finch wings
recovering after the surgeon's laser
sliced through my abdomen,
maneuvering the DaVinci robot
to remove the organs of my making.
Why does hysterectomy begin
with its mouth open to scream?

The utter yellow gleam of the meteor broke
subarctic night, rocked boulders
for miles as schoolchildren pressed
noses flat to see this burning angel
hiss past their history class before they screeched,
small owls terrified of brilliance shot
from outer space or the hand of God
that once sanctified tyrant tsars.

I listen for morning birds. A goldfinch can break
my heart with its song alone, the wheeze
so plaintive; it charms the rain
from clouds that numb desert dawn.

BURYING HAPPY

Together we lower the white wolf
into black river bottom soil, cover
his guard hairs, his spiritual face
with sheepskin, arrange his stuffed rhino toy,
Milk Bones, ginger snaps, chicken thighs,
a beef shank and bits of ground buffalo
near his stilled thick jaws
that could crack a wrestler's arm bone,
his perfect onyx lips.

      Never was a wolf more handsome, eyeliner
black as Ramses around dark honey-colored eyes,
legs long for leaping blue snow banks, paws
nearly as big as my hands. Happy. Bill's happiness
sunk into fertile earth
under the pear tree that will be the first
to blossom in our yard
come spring.

      Oh, white wolf, just a month shy of fourteen,
how many years you dolphined through drifts
or swam powerful as a polar bear
paddling across the deep blue reservoir's end.

      White wolf, love groomed you from your white claws
to your wide smile to ears white-furred, standing alert to
catch the finest birdsong and plant-stir of pine forest.
Light stretches each of my ribs
from the inside-out with indelible longing, a sea

of never wanting to say goodbye, even
though goodbye is the Universal translator
we all must learn to speak, a sort of grace,
the soft eider under the primaries of an eagle
as it screams hunting from sky
or the cry of a fawn for its mother
stepping into the path of the mountain lion
who lives on the ridge above our house.

Early from Mexico, redwing blackbirds have returned,
spread red epaulets on inky shoulders
waiting weeks for their mates
on cattails they've staked out
in the barrow ditch along the road.

                    Oh, Happy, I see your legs stretch
shoot like moonlight down the road,
fast beside Bill's car, inhaling
lungs full of the mountain air you were born to.

I have no doubt you cured me
of cancer, took it on, although there will be those
who'll laugh at my claim.

It was your great pink tongue
that licked tears from my cheeks
after my brother died, after
domestic strife stupified our house.
Circling the welcome mat, you waited
faithful through the night against
the blue door of our sorrow for Bill,
your soul-friend to come home.

Remember the steady strokes along your ears,
the way Bill curled like a fern around you,
holding you against pain, the whispered secrets
and my kisses balanced on your strong cheek bones
under thick Arctic fur.

Your eyes seldom left Bill walking,
writing poems, throwing stick
after stick in deep water
                    For you, only you, dear Happy,
so immense his complete adoration
deep as the gorge that cuts
through the Weminuche all the way to Granite Peak.

When Lulu, your red wolf mate, suddenly died
the night after she lie on the rug,
her entire spine pressed
into the length of yours,
                    you howled a lonesome year
just as I grieve for you now,
snow wolf howling at the edge
of the frigid river, at the edge of the sea,
white wolf, you
who rubbbed your muzzle
nightly on all of us, on the hand-woven rug
we shared beside a fire, dreaming
while the fierce winds of the world blew on.

AUTUMN ECLIPSE

Even behind the slush of clouds
you know the moon is full.
Your heart is a familiar well
the world falls through.
No wind sweeps night
but walnut fronds drop
like snapped wings.
You remember a fondness
for sunny stumps, the lonely
smell of lightning-felled trees,
a clearing in the woods
where you picked Bergamot
and Forget-Me-Nots
that wilted before dusk.
Everything is going fine,
no hitches, just middle age.

Bear and swan disappear
from the sad amphitheatre of sky
and what you hear is the swamp
attended by a gushing flume.
You might mistake a shadow
for a bittern, its head
thrown back, camouflaged
by upthrust reeds.
Everything is a quick ghost,
even your feet, kicking
through memory, unbidden leaves
falling from dreams,

the still-green stalks of lilies
gone to seed, raspberry
bramble, cranberry bog,
lamb's tongue, goldenrod,
slabs of wet blue slate, back
to the glaciated land
you grew up with.

You see again the sudden owl,
eyes red spears, wings
on fire, trailing sparks
into the dry woods
the day you became a woman.
Bloody coals blew to flame.

You can feel the moon,
the shadow of your own earth
pulling across its broad silver.
Even treefrogs cease
their harmonic thrum
while geese oboe south
through the echoing sky
until there is nothing
but the empty cover
of your skin, softening.

More manic in this silence,
the flume bursts its course
and you laugh at the mechanics of fate,
the way, no matter how far you travel,
you always come back to this—
the world swallowed gradually by dark,
its dramatic recovery. Light.

FAITH

for Regina de Cormier (*In Memorium*)

I

Some nights everything hangs
from the hooks of faith,
even the moon, old
hatchetface, cheesy blade
flat as a gravedigger's shovel.
You are every woman who writes
against silence so huge
your heart is volatile as gasoline
at desert noon that explodes
each ring of language
conceived by your blood.

You're alone so often that
the keys of your typewriter knock
like an engine about to throw a rod,
and every image is a broken tooth
cutting your mouth or an arm
that hugs your stomach warm
in a dream of the present time
you had as a child.

II

Once in a bad time, a friend advised,
      "Your work is your angel."
Sometimes the heart is that angel
stepping from Dante's flames.

"I must get on with my burning," she cries
as the crepe wings char.

Woman, you compose poems
stealing fire from the sun
held hostage by some invisible coast
until the flame-blue pony of imagination
bolts, hauling misery from your bones.
Outside of connections and literary parties, you
compose in your heart, where
poured steel and honey conjure song.

III

Some days sky fades to the color of axes
and abused aluminum pots
as it drags its fingernails across the roof
and nothing appears in the mail
but debts. You watch
smoke seep from your fingertips
as dusk takes your last cigarette.

It is then you're plagued by the fly,
its fat black legs ripped
from last summer's moon
that still buzzes your studio.
Greasy glutton of windowsills, it
sticks to your hair, bumps your forehead
with its inevitable thud.
You wonder at this discordant singer
with its thousand-paned eyes,
its ultrahuman sight,
lyric thief, sweat monger,

Emerald common as bread,
a quivering brooch even the poor
whose lives you champion,
can afford.

IV

Playing with Oscar,
the tiger-striped puppy, I understand
what real poets learn.
Over and over, he fetches a tennis ball,
tooth-pocked and dripping spit.
His delight is total,
faith inexhaustible as his love
when he drops the ball at my feet.
Grinning above black lips,
his eyes dilate into gold flames
until I throw it, and he spins
across the lawn, all electric leap,
then snaps it up neat in his white teeth
to offer the prize for another toss.
I love his wide laughter,
unquenchable desire.

It isn't the ball but
the language singing between
my hand and his mouth
that consumes him.
It is new for him every time.
Every time this unabashed communion
of infinite familiarity and variety
ending in joy.

V

A blue map of the world is pinned
like a porthole to my wall.
On it I mark where friends, scattered
across the continent, write.
On the opposite coast, snow
breaks from Montreal
to Manhattan, breaks over you
who have such a hard time staying warm.
I know how the storm will drive
its fists into your heart, blasting
any new blooms.

I send this poem, a charm
to shatter weather and distance
for all women who write
against the silent ear of the world,
a charm of blood and memory
to break the indifferent blade
of tonight's moon.
Faith is as simple as dreams.
Regina, your one sure power is
language that feeds all need.

I close my eyes and hear
your songs magnify the lunar tide,
oldest of sisters, that
muses just beyond my door.

ACKNOWLEDGMENTS

MAGAZINES

Arabesques International: "A Siberian Cold Front Takes Over the
Last Week of April" (Algeria, reprint)

Big River Poetry Reivew: "Knowing The Enemy"

The Bloomsbury Review: "Banking the Fire"

Calyx: "Brewing Borscht" and "Ferry Shelling"

Charlie Mike: "The Trick" (reprint)

Cimmarron Review: "Parachute"

Commonweal: "Red Cat Near Old Snow"

Connotation Press: "There Are No Inlaws In This Poem" and
"Night Terrors"

In The Fray: "Operation Iraqi Freedom Ends"

Iris: "Faith" (Iris Poetry Prize, University of Virginia)

The Malahat Review: "Long Distance Home" (Canada)

The Mas Tequila Review: "The Dead Unburied by Spring"

Naugatuck Review: "French Horn"

New Millenium: "Shostakovich: Five Pieces" (2010 *New
Millenium Poetry Prize*) and "Learning the Theremin;"
reprinted from winning writers.com, "Horoscope," "White
Phosphorous at Hanukkah," and "The Taliban Takes Pakistan"
(2011 War Poetry Prize from www.winningwriters.com)

Nimrod: "The Trick" and "A Dream, My Child"

Out of Line: "Erasing the Names"

Parnassus Review Of Poetry: "Red Menace" and "A Siberian Cold
Front Takes Over The Last Week Of April"

Peregrine: "June's Hottest Day"

Ploughshares: "Remembering the TET Offensive as I Watch
Troops Ship Out for a U.S. Attack on Iraq"

Poems & Plays, Last Call: "Genesis Revised: The Chernobyl
Buffaloes"

Poet & Critic: "Ruined Honey"
Poetry: "After Reading Louise Bogan's Journals"
Poetry Miscellany: "Spotting Whoopers"
Saxifrage: "Talk About Your Bad Girls" (Editor's Choice Award, titled "Reunion")
Taos Journal of Poetry: "Iron and Lace" and "Meteoric"
The Tucson Poet: "The Trick" (reprint)
Valparaiso Review: "Another Easter Snowstorm" (poem of the month)
Zone: "Wildflowers"

ANTHOLOGIES

Bridges: Poets of the Hudson Valley, ed. David Appelbaum and Regina de Cormier, "Autumn Eclipse"
Fathers, ed. David and Judy Ray, "Long Distance Home"
Only Morning in Her Shoes: "Wildflowers"
Poets Against the War: "Remembering the TET Offensive as I Watch Troops Ship Out for a U.S. Attack on Iraq" (online)

CHAPBOOKS

"Talk About Your Bad Girls" ("Reunion") was published in *WITHOUT BIRDS, WITHOUT FLOWERS, WITHOUT TREES*, winner of the 1990 Flume Press Chapbook Award, chosen by Linda Hogan.

"Red Menace," "A Siberian Cold Front Takes Over the Last Week of April," "Black Swan," "Brewing Borscht," "Red Cat Near Old Snow," and "Bloodflower," appeared in the online chapbook, *BLOOD FLOWER*, published by Rebecca Seiferle in *the drunken boat.com*

Thank you to all my friends and family who believe in me and who love me, inspire me and who push me to be better than I ever hoped to be despite my cracks and flaws. Special thanks to Lynn and Donley Watt, Rick Jackson, Terry Harvey, Marilyn Kallet, Alfred Corn, Teri Hairston, Charlotte Lowe, Cynthia Hogue, Linda Hogan, Karen Brennan, TR Hummer, Albert Kogel, Ken Stahl, Jerry Gates, Larry and Ellen Hartsfied, all my nieces and nephews, my cousins, all my students around the country, Dick and Gay Grossman, Arnold and Marilyn Nelson, Fox McGrew, Doug and Andrea Peacock, Naomi Shihab Nye, Carmen Calata-yud, Darryl Klesch, Diana Hadley, and in memorium to my Aunt Olga Moberg, Peter Warshall, Doug and Richard Rockefeller, And, huge thanks to my publisher and friend, Bryce Milligan, who works so hard and long to keep poetry alive and well in our world.

ABOUT THE AUTHOR

Like Lorca, Uschuk is a poet of the duende, that mystical Spanish conception; she views the poem as a vehicle for fierce engagement with the body and its social realities, often with a metaphysical awareness that transcends and extends the corporeal into the natural world. Working a poetics rare for a North American writer, Uschuk has crafted a poetry equally steeped in nature and political resistance. This is an ecological poetics of engagement, a mythic poetry—part Lorca, part Rachel Carson.

—Sean Thomas Dougherty,
Rain Taxi, 2012

Political activist and wilderness advocate, Pam Uschuk has howled out six books of poems, including *Crazy Love,* winner of a 2010 American Book Award, *Wild in the Plaza of Memory*, and now *Blood Flower.*

Translated into a dozen languages, her work appears in over three hundred journals and anthologies worldwide, including *Poetry, Ploughshares, Agni Review,* etc.

Uschuk has been awarded the 2011 War Poetry Prize from *Winning Writers*, 2010 New Millenium Poetry Prize, 2010 Best of the Web, the Struga International Poetry Prize (for a theme poem), the Dorothy Daniels Writing Award from the National League of American PEN Women, the King's English Poetry Prize and prizes from *Ascent, Iris,* and *Amnesty International.*

An associate Professor of Creative Writing at Fort Lewis College and the Editor-In-Chief of *Cutthroat, A Journal of the Arts,* Uschuk lives in Bayfield, Colorado. Uschuk is often a featured writer at the Prague Summer Programs, and was the 2011 John C. Hodges Visiting Writer at University of Tennessee, Knoxville. She's working on a multi-genre book called "The Book of Healers Healing; An Odyssey through Ovarian Cancer."

Wings Press was founded in 1975 by Joanie Whitebird and Joseph F. Lomax, both deceased, as "an informal association of artists and cultural mythologists dedicated to the preservation of the literature of the nation of Texas." Publisher, editor and designer since 1995, Bryce Milligan is honored to carry on and expand that mission to include the finest in American writing—meaning all of the Americas, without commercial considerations clouding the decision to publish or not to publish.

Wings Press publishes multi-cultural books, chapbooks, ebooks, recordings and broadsides that, we hope, enlighten the human spirit and enliven the mind. Everyone ever associated with Wings has been or is a writer, and we know well that writing is a transformational art form capable of changing the world, primarily by allowing us to glimpse something of each other's souls. We believe that good writing is innovative, insightful, and interesting. But most of all it is honest. As Bob Dylan put it, "To live outside the law, you must be honest." Likewise, Wings Press is committed to treating the planet itself as a partner. Thus the press uses as much recycled material as possible, from the paper on which the books are printed to the boxes in which they are shipped.

As Robert Dana wrote in *Against the Grain,* "Small press publishing is personal publishing. In essence, it's a matter of personal vision, personal taste and courage, and personal friendships." Welcome to our world.

WINGS PRESS

Colophon

This first edition of *Blood Flower*, by Pamela Uschuk, has been printed on 55 pound Edwards Brothers Natural Paper containing a percentage of recycled fiber. Titles have been set in Flat Bush and Charlemagne type, the text in Adobe Caslon type. All Wings Press books are designed and produced by Bryce Milligan.

On-line catalogue and ordering:
www.wingspress.com

Wings Press titles are distributed
to the trade by the
Independent Publishers Group
www.ipgbook.com
and in Europe by
www.gazellebookservices.co.uk

Also available as an ebook.